I'M 9, EVERYTHING'S FINE
MAD LIBS

by Ellen Lee

MAD LIBS
An imprint of Penguin Random House LLC, New York

First published in the United States of America by Mad Libs,
an imprint of Penguin Random House LLC, New York, 2023

Mad Libs format and text copyright © 2023 by Penguin Random House LLC

Concept created by Roger Price & Leonard Stern

Cover illustration by Scott Brooks

Penguin supports copyright. Copyright fuels creativity, encourages diverse voices,
promotes free speech, and creates a vibrant culture. Thank you for buying an authorized
edition of this book and for complying with copyright laws by not reproducing, scanning,
or distributing any part of it in any form without permission. You are supporting writers
and allowing Penguin to continue to publish books for every reader.

MAD LIBS and logo are registered trademarks of Penguin Random House LLC.

Visit us online at penguinrandomhouse.com.

Printed in the United States of America

ISBN 9780593523193
1 3 5 7 9 10 8 6 4 2
COMR

MAD⊙LIBS®

INSTRUCTIONS

MAD LIBS® is a game for people who don't like games!
It can be played by one, two, three, four, or forty.

● RIDICULOUSLY SIMPLE DIRECTIONS

In this tablet you will find stories containing blank spaces where words
are left out. One player, the READER, selects one of these stories. The
READER does not tell anyone what the story is about. Instead, he/she asks
the other players, the WRITERS, to give him/her words. These words are
used to fill in the blank spaces in the story.

● TO PLAY

The READER asks each WRITER in turn to call out a word—an adjective or
a noun or whatever the space calls for—and uses them to fill in the blank
spaces in the story. The result is a MAD LIBS® game.

When the READER then reads the completed MAD LIBS® game to the other
players, they will discover that they have written a story that is fantastic,
screamingly funny, shocking, silly, crazy, or just plain dumb—depending
upon which words each WRITER called out.

● EXAMPLE (*Before* and *After*)

"_____ !" he said _____
                EXCLAMATION   ADVERB

as he jumped into his convertible _____ and
                                                    NOUN

drove off with his _____ wife.
                            ADJECTIVE

"_____**OUCH**_____ !" he said _____**HAPPILY**_____
          EXCLAMATION   ADVERB

as he jumped into his convertible _____**CAT**_____ and
                                              NOUN

drove off with his _____**BRAVE**_____ wife.
                          ADJECTIVE

In case you have forgotten what adjectives, adverbs, nouns, and verbs are, here is a quick review:

An ADJECTIVE describes something or somebody. *Lumpy, soft, ugly, messy,* and *short* are adjectives.

An ADVERB tells how something is done. It modifies a verb and usually ends in "ly." *Modestly, stupidly, greedily,* and *carefully* are adverbs.

A NOUN is the name of a person, place, or thing. *Sidewalk, umbrella, bridle, bathtub,* and *nose* are nouns.

A VERB is an action word. *Run, pitch, jump,* and *swim* are verbs. Put the verbs in past tense if the directions say PAST TENSE. *Ran, pitched, jumped,* and *swam* are verbs in the past tense.

When we ask for A PLACE, we mean any sort of place: a country or city (*Spain, Cleveland*) or a room (*bathroom, kitchen*).

An EXCLAMATION or SILLY WORD is any sort of funny sound, gasp, grunt, or outcry, like *Wow!, Ouch!, Whomp!, Ick!,* and *Gadzooks!*

When we ask for specific words, like a NUMBER, a COLOR, an ANIMAL, or a PART OF THE BODY, we mean a word that is one of those things, like *seven, blue, horse,* or *head.*

When we ask for a PLURAL, it means more than one. For example, *cat* pluralized is *cats.*

MAD LIBS® is fun to play with friends, but you can also play it by yourself! To begin with, DO NOT look at the story on the page below. Fill in the blanks on this page with the words called for. Then, using the words you have selected, fill in the blank spaces in the story.

Now you've created your own hilarious MAD LIBS® game!

I'M 9, I'M SO FINE!

NUMBER _____

ANIMAL _____

NOUN _____

A PLACE _____

VERB _____

TYPE OF LIQUID _____

VEHICLE _____

COUNTRY _____

ADJECTIVE _____

VERB ENDING IN "ING" _____

PERSON YOU KNOW _____

ARTICLE OF CLOTHING _____

YOUR NAME _____

CELEBRITY _____

TYPE OF EVENT _____

TYPE OF BUILDING _____

SILLY WORD _____

MAD LIBS®

I'M 9, I'M SO FINE!

I've been waiting _____ long years to be nine! Being nine is like
                        NUMBER

being the top _____ in the animal kingdom. The largest
                    ANIMAL

_____ in the food chain. The biggest, baddest beast in (the)
    NOUN

_____ . Being nine means I am old enough to _____
    A PLACE   VERB

all day and all night! I can drink all the _____ I want! I
                                                TYPE OF LIQUID

can even drive my _____ all the way to _____
                        VEHICLE   COUNTRY

if I feel like it. I have huge _____ plans for being nine. I'm
                                    ADJECTIVE

going to practice _____ every day. In a few weeks,
                    VERB ENDING IN "ING"

I'm going to climb to the snowy peak of Mt. _____ .
                                                PERSON YOU KNOW

And I'm going to start a new _____ line called House
                                ARTICLE OF CLOTHING

of _____ . _____ will wear my designs on the red
    YOUR NAME   CELEBRITY

carpet for the annual _____ gala at the _____ .
                        TYPE OF EVENT   TYPE OF BUILDING

I am nine, hear me roar: " _____ !"
                            SILLY WORD

From I'M 9, EVERYTHING'S FINE MAD LIBS® • Copyright © 2023 by Penguin Random House LLC

MAD LIBS® is fun to play with friends, but you can also play it by yourself! To begin with, DO NOT look at the story on the page below. Fill in the blanks on this page with the words called for. Then, using the words you have selected, fill in the blank spaces in the story.

Now you've created your own hilarious MAD LIBS® game!

SLIME TIME

OCCUPATION _____

NUMBER _____

TYPE OF BUILDING _____

PART OF THE BODY _____

PERSON YOU KNOW _____

ADJECTIVE _____

VERB ENDING IN "ING" _____

TYPE OF CONTAINER _____

NUMBER _____

TYPE OF FOOD _____

NOUN _____

SILLY WORD _____

COLOR _____

TYPE OF LIQUID _____

PART OF THE BODY _____

NUMBER _____

ARTICLE OF CLOTHING _____

PART OF THE BODY _____

SLIME TIME

You don't need to be a/an _____ to make slime! All you
OCCUPATION

need is _____ ingredients you can find in any _____.
NUMBER   TYPE OF BUILDING

1. Grab a bottle of _____ shampoo from _____.
   PART OF THE BODY   PERSON YOU KNOW

   If you want to make your slime extra _____ , borrow
                                          ADJECTIVE

   some _____ cream instead.
        VERB ENDING IN "ING"

2. Pour the liquid into a large _____ . Add _____
                                TYPE OF CONTAINER   NUMBER

   tablespoons of _____ -starch. Don't add too much
                   TYPE OF FOOD

   _____ —it will make your mixture go _____!
   NOUN   SILLY WORD

3. Squeeze three drops of _____ _____ into
                          COLOR   TYPE OF LIQUID

   the mixture and knead with your _____ for at least
                                    PART OF THE BODY

   _____ minutes. Warning: Slime is messy, so wear an old
   NUMBER

   _____ over your _____!
   ARTICLE OF CLOTHING   PART OF THE BODY

From I'M 9, EVERYTHING'S FINE MAD LIBS® • Copyright © 2023 by Penguin Random House LLC

MAD LIBS® is fun to play with friends, but you can also play it by yourself! To begin with, DO NOT look at the story on the page below. Fill in the blanks on this page with the words called for. Then, using the words you have selected, fill in the blank spaces in the story.

Now you've created your own hilarious MAD LIBS® game!

THAT TIME MY BFF SLEEP OVER

PERSON YOU KNOW _____

ADJECTIVE _____

TYPE OF FOOD _____

PLURAL NOUN _____

ADJECTIVE _____

ADJECTIVE _____

TYPE OF CONTAINER _____

SOMETHING ALIVE _____

SILLY WORD _____

SAME SILLY WORD _____

VERB ENDING IN "ING" _____

ARTICLE OF CLOTHING (PLURAL) _____

CELEBRITY _____

NOUN _____

TYPE OF FOOD _____

VERB _____

PLURAL NOUN _____

ADJECTIVE _____

MAD LIBS
THAT TIME MY BFF SLEPT OVER

Whenever my BFF, _____, sleeps over, we always have
　　　　　　　　　PERSON YOU KNOW

the most _____ time. We make sure we have a generous
　　　　　ADJECTIVE

supply of yummy _____ to snack on, and we stay up late
　　　　　　　　TYPE OF FOOD

watching our favorite movie, *The Secret Life of* _____.
　　　　　　　　　　　　　　　　　　　　　　　　　PLURAL NOUN

I'll never forget our most _____ sleepover. That night,
　　　　　　　　　　　　　ADJECTIVE

we heard strange, _____ sounds coming from outside
　　　　　　　　　ADJECTIVE

my _____. At first, we thought it was just a/an
　　TYPE OF CONTAINER

_____ rustling in the wind. Then someone started
SOMETHING ALIVE

moaning, "_____ _____." We were so scared
　　　　　SILLY WORD　　　SAME SILLY WORD

we were _____ in our _____.
　　　VERB ENDING IN "ING"　　　ARTICLE OF CLOTHING (PLURAL)

Out of nowhere, a ghost that looked eerily like _____
　　　　　　　　　　　　　　　　　　　　　　CELEBRITY

floated in front of us and said, "I am your worst _____.
　　　　　　　　　　　　　　　　　　　　　　　　　NOUN

Give me all your _____ or I'll _____ you!"
　　　　　　　TYPE OF FOOD　　　　　　VERB

We screamed and turned on the _____. It turned out
　　　　　　　　　　　　　　　PLURAL NOUN

the ghost was just my _____ brother!
　　　　　　　　　ADJECTIVE

From I'M 9, EVERYTHING'S FINE MAD LIBS® • Copyright © 2023 by Penguin Random House LLC

MAD LIBS® is fun to play with friends, but you can also play it by yourself! To begin with, DO NOT look at the story on the page below. Fill in the blanks on this page with the words called for. Then, using the words you have selected, fill in the blank spaces in the story.

Now you've created your own hilarious MAD LIBS® game!

SCREEN TIME RULES

PLURAL NOUN _____

NOUN _____

ADJECTIVE _____

NUMBER _____

VERB ENDING IN "ING" _____

ADJECTIVE _____

NUMBER _____

TYPE OF LIQUID _____

VERB _____

TYPE OF FOOD _____

ADJECTIVE _____

CELEBRITY _____

ADJECTIVE _____

ANIMAL (PLURAL) _____

PART OF THE BODY (PLURAL) _____

PERSON YOU KNOW _____

MAD LIBS®

SCREEN TIME RULES

To my loving, caring _____,
PLURAL NOUN

Now that I am nine years old, I am so ready to have my own smart-

_____ . I promise to always follow your _____
NOUN   ADJECTIVE

rules. I will stare at it for only _____ hours each day. I also
NUMBER

promise to spend plenty of time _____ outdoors,
VERB ENDING IN "ING"

reading _____ books, and finishing my _____
ADJECTIVE   NUMBER

chores. I will be careful and won't accidentally drop the phone in

_____ or recklessly _____ with it. I will put it
TYPE OF LIQUID   VERB

away whenever we are eating _____ during dinner. At
TYPE OF FOOD

bedtime, I will shut my phone off and ignore all _____
ADJECTIVE

messages, even if it is an emergency and _____ needs my
CELEBRITY

help. I will definitely not waste my time watching _____
ADJECTIVE

videos of _____ chasing their _____ .
ANIMAL (PLURAL)   PART OF THE BODY (PLURAL)

No, all I'll do is use it to keep in touch with you and my bestie,

_____ .
PERSON YOU KNOW

From I'M 9, EVERYTHING'S FINE MAD LIBS® • Copyright © 2023 by Penguin Random House LLC

MAD LIBS® is fun to play with friends, but you can also play it by yourself! To begin with, DO NOT look at the story on the page below. Fill in the blanks on this page with the words called for. Then, using the words you have selected, fill in the blank spaces in the story.

Now you've created your own hilarious MAD LIBS® game!

SUMMER PLANS

ADJECTIVE _____

TYPE OF FOOD _____

ANIMAL (PLURAL) _____

CELEBRITY _____

TYPE OF BUILDING _____

VERB _____

ADJECTIVE _____

PERSON YOU KNOW _____

NUMBER _____

VERB ENDING IN "ING" _____

TYPE OF LIQUID _____

SOMETHING ALIVE (PLURAL) _____

OCCUPATION _____

NOUN _____

CELEBRITY _____

ARTICLE OF CLOTHING (PLURAL) _____

A PLACE _____

MAD LIBS®

SUMMER PLANS

Take this _____ quiz to find out what to do this summer:
     ADJECTIVE

1. What would you do if you had a/an _____ tree? (a) help
                                          TYPE OF FOOD

    feed hungry _____ , (b) hire _____
              ANIMAL (PLURAL)   CELEBRITY

    to make a commercial so you can sell _____-made
                                          TYPE OF BUILDING

    pies on TV, (c) climb the tree and _____ in it
                                              VERB

2. What is your _____ hobby? (a) hanging out with
                     ADJECTIVE

    _____ , of course! (b) making _____ dollars,
    PERSON YOU KNOW   NUMBER

    (c) _____ in cool _____
        VERB ENDING IN "ING"   TYPE OF LIQUID

If you answered both questions with *a*'s: Start a committee to save

the _____ . If you answered both questions with
    SOMETHING ALIVE (PLURAL)

b's: Become the _____ of a new company and take
                      OCCUPATION

over the _____ with _____ . If you answered
            NOUN   CELEBRITY

both questions with *c*'s: Pack up your _____
                                        ARTICLE OF CLOTHING (PLURAL)

and take a vacation to (the) _____ .
                                A PLACE

From I'M 9, EVERYTHING'S FINE MAD LIBS® • Copyright © 2023 by Penguin Random House LLC

MAD LIBS® is fun to play with friends, but you can also play it by yourself! To begin with, DO NOT look at the story on the page below. Fill in the blanks on this page with the words called for. Then, using the words you have selected, fill in the blank spaces in the story.

Now you've created your own hilarious MAD LIBS® game!

SUPER SPY

TYPE OF FOOD _____

NOUN _____

TYPE OF CONTAINER _____

TYPE OF BUILDING _____

PERSON YOU KNOW _____

PART OF THE BODY (PLURAL) _____

COLOR _____

ARTICLE OF CLOTHING (PLURAL) _____

TYPE OF LIQUID _____

PART OF THE BODY _____

NOUN _____

ADJECTIVE _____

PART OF THE BODY _____

SILLY WORD _____

ANIMAL (PLURAL) _____

SOMETHING ALIVE _____

EXCLAMATION _____

TYPE OF EVENT _____

MAD LIBS®

SUPER SPY

The other day, I noticed some pretty strange things happening at the

_____ restaurant down the street. All morning long, people
   TYPE OF FOOD

were carrying a/an _____-shaped _____ in and
             NOUN   TYPE OF CONTAINER

out of the _____. It was time for _____
        TYPE OF BUILDING   PERSON YOU KNOW

and me to go undercover and investigate. We put on our disguises:

large fake _____, _____ wigs,
        PART OF THE BODY (PLURAL)   COLOR

and camouflage _____. We packed a bag with
           ARTICLE OF CLOTHING (PLURAL)

invisible _____, a/an _____-print kit, and
       TYPE OF LIQUID   PART OF THE BODY

a spy camera that looked like a/an _____. We practiced our
                                NOUN

secret _____ signals: If we saw something suspicious, we
      ADJECTIVE

wiggled our _____. Our code word, if we got into
        PART OF THE BODY

serious trouble and needed help, was "_____." We were
                            SILLY WORD

as quiet as _____ as we tiptoed inside. I ducked behind
        ANIMAL (PLURAL)

a/an _____ and slowly peeked out. _____!
    SOMETHING ALIVE   EXCLAMATION

It was a surprise _____—for me!
        TYPE OF EVENT

From I'M 9, EVERYTHING'S FINE MAD LIBS® • Copyright © 2023 by Penguin Random House LLC

MAD LIBS® is fun to play with friends, but you can also play it by yourself! To begin with, DO NOT look at the story on the page below. Fill in the blanks on this page with the words called for. Then, using the words you have selected, fill in the blank spaces in the story.

Now you've created your own hilarious MAD LIBS® game!

INSIDE THE PIÑATA

PLURAL NOUN _____

TYPE OF FOOD _____

ANIMAL _____

PART OF THE BODY _____

CELEBRITY _____

NOUN _____

SOMETHING ALIVE _____

PERSON YOU KNOW _____

VERB _____

NOUN _____

PART OF THE BODY (PLURAL) _____

ARTICLE OF CLOTHING _____

SILLY WORD _____

TYPE OF FOOD (PLURAL) _____

ADJECTIVE _____

ANIMAL _____

ADJECTIVE _____

EXCLAMATION _____

INSIDE THE PIÑATA

You never know what kind of awesome _____ might come
_____PLURAL NOUN

out of a piñata. I like the _____-flavored lollipops and
_____TYPE OF FOOD

_____-shaped chocolates the most. Sometimes there will be
ANIMAL

little toys, like stickers you can stick on your _____.
_____PART OF THE BODY

But one time, something awful happened at _____'s
_____CELEBRITY

birthday party. A colorful _____-shaped pinata was hung
NOUN

from a/an _____. _____ and I couldn't wait
SOMETHING ALIVE   PERSON YOU KNOW

to _____ the piñata with a big _____. We
VERB   NOUN

each took turns covering our _____ with a/an
_____PART OF THE BODY (PLURAL)

_____ and giving the piñata a good, solid _____.
ARTICLE OF CLOTHING   SILLY WORD

But when we finally broke open the piñata, the only things that fell

out were half-eaten _____ and _____ candy
_____TYPE OF FOOD (PLURAL)   ADJECTIVE

wrappers! It turned out a mischievous little _____ had
ANIMAL

gotten into the piñata and eaten all the _____ treats.
ADJECTIVE

_____!
EXCLAMATION

From I'M 9, EVERYTHING'S FINE MAD LIBS® • Copyright © 2023 by Penguin Random House LLC

MAD LIBS® is fun to play with friends, but you can also play it by yourself! To begin with, DO NOT look at the story on the page below. Fill in the blanks on this page with the words called for. Then, using the words you have selected, fill in the blank spaces in the story.

Now you've created your own hilarious MAD LIBS® game!

WARRIOR CHALLENGE

NUMBER _____

ADJECTIVE _____

PERSON YOU KNOW _____

PART OF THE BODY _____

NOUN _____

ANIMAL _____

PLURAL NOUN _____

PART OF THE BODY _____

PLURAL NOUN _____

VERB ENDING IN "ING" _____

TYPE OF LIQUID _____

CELEBRITY _____

VERB _____

COLOR _____

EXCLAMATION _____

NUMBER _____

SILLY WORD _____

I've been training _____ hours every day for the annual
NUMBER

_____ Warrior Challenge! _____ has been
ADJECTIVE   PERSON YOU KNOW

helping me get my _____ in tip-top shape, cheering
PART OF THE BODY

me on with motivational messages like "No _____, no
NOUN

gain!" On the day of the race, I feel as strong and as nimble as a/an

_____. I sprint up the first obstacle course and make
ANIMAL

a flying leap to grab the skinny metal _____. My
PLURAL NOUN

_____ almost slips but I hang on—barely. Next, I scramble
PART OF THE BODY

through the maze of razor-sharp _____ and dodge the
PLURAL NOUN

_____ rubber balls. For the final obstacle course, I
VERB ENDING IN "ING"

have to climb up the tower of terror as hot _____ rains
TYPE OF LIQUID

down on me. From behind, I can see _____ gaining on me,
CELEBRITY

but I _____ as hard as I can and slam the _____
VERB   COLOR

buzzer. _____! I completed the entire course in a record-
EXCLAMATION

breaking _____ minutes. Say "_____" to your
NUMBER   SILLY WORD

new Warrior Challenge winner!

From I'M 9, EVERYTHING'S FINE MAD LIBS® • Copyright © 2023 by Penguin Random House LLC

MAD LIBS® is fun to play with friends, but you can also play it by yourself! To begin with, DO NOT look at the story on the page below. Fill in the blanks on this page with the words called for. Then, using the words you have selected, fill in the blank spaces in the story.

Now you've created your own hilarious MAD LIBS® game!

ANNUAL CHECKUP

OCCUPATION _____

LAST NAME _____

NUMBER _____

PART OF THE BODY _____

NOUN _____

PART OF THE BODY _____

SILLY WORD _____

PART OF THE BODY _____

LETTER OF THE ALPHABET _____

NOUN _____

ANIMAL (PLURAL) _____

NUMBER _____

EXCLAMATION _____

TYPE OF FOOD _____

TYPE OF LIQUID _____

TYPE OF FOOD _____

VERB ENDING IN "ING" _____

MAD LIBS

ANNUAL CHECKUP

It's time for my annual checkup with the _____. First
OCCUPATION

Dr. _____ takes my temperature, which is a normal
LAST NAME

_____ degrees. Then the doctor listens to my _____
NUMBER   PART OF THE BODY

with a stethoscope. "Hmmm," the doctor says. "It sounds like your

heart is beating to the rhythm of the _____." Next,
NOUN

the doctor tells me to stick out my _____ and say
PART OF THE BODY

"_____!" I also cover one _____ at a time
SILLY WORD   PART OF THE BODY

and read the letters on the eye chart. My doctor is amazed when I can

even read the tiny letter _____ on the bottom of the
LETTER OF THE ALPHABET

_____. During the hearing test, I can hear high-pitched
NOUN

sounds that only _____ can hear. And in the past
ANIMAL (PLURAL)

year, I grew more than _____ inches. "_____! You
NUMBER   EXCLAMATION

must be eating lots of healthy _____ and drinking lots of
TYPE OF FOOD

fortified _____!" the doctor says. "Well, actually," I reply,
TYPE OF LIQUID

"I mostly eat _____! But I have been _____
TYPE OF FOOD   VERB ENDING IN "ING"

daily!"

From I'M 9, EVERYTHING'S FINE MAD LIBS® • Copyright © 2023 by Penguin Random House LLC

MAD LIBS® is fun to play with friends, but you can also play it by yourself! To begin with, DO NOT look at the story on the page below. Fill in the blanks on this page with the words called for. Then, using the words you have selected, fill in the blank spaces in the story.

Now you've created your own hilarious MAD LIBS® game!

MAD SCIENTISTS

EXCLAMATION _____

ADJECTIVE _____

TYPE OF LIQUID _____

COLOR _____

TYPE OF FOOD _____

PART OF THE BODY _____

ANIMAL _____

ARTICLE OF CLOTHING _____

CELEBRITY _____

NUMBER _____

TYPE OF LIQUID _____

SOMETHING ALIVE _____

NOUN _____

ADJECTIVE _____

VERB _____

SILLY WORD _____

SAME SILLY WORD _____

MAD LIBS®

MAD SCIENTISTS

Inside the lab of two mad scientists:

Marie: _____! Let's make our _____ potion!
　　　　　　EXCLAMATION　　　　　　　　　　　　ADJECTIVE

Pierre: Okay! Is the _____ bubbling?
　　　　　　　　　　　　TYPE OF LIQUID

Marie: Yes! It's completely _____ and tastes as sweet as
　　　　　　　　　　　　　　　　　　COLOR

_____.
TYPE OF FOOD

Pierre: Great! I'll add some hair from the _____ of a/an
　　　　　　　　　　　　　　　　　　　　　PART OF THE BODY

_____.
ANIMAL

Marie: And don't forget the _____ from _____
　　　　　　　　　　　　　ARTICLE OF CLOTHING　　　　　　CELEBRITY

that's been worn for at least _____ days in a row.
　　　　　　　　　　　　　　NUMBER

Pierre: Got it! Next, we add one drop of _____ from a/an
　　　　　　　　　　　　　　　　　　　TYPE OF LIQUID

_____ that was collected on the first night of the full
SOMETHING ALIVE

_____.
NOUN

Marie: This potion is going to be _____! Everyone who
　　　　　　　　　　　　　　　　　ADJECTIVE

drinks it will _____ whenever someone says _____!
　　　　　　　VERB　　　　　　　　　　　　　　　　　SILLY WORD

Pierre: Bwa-ha-ha-_____! We are the most brilliant mad
　　　　　　　　　　SAME SILLY WORD

scientists!

From I'M 9, EVERYTHING'S FINE MAD LIBS® • Copyright © 2023 by Penguin Random House LLC

MAD LIBS® is fun to play with friends, but you can also play it by yourself! To begin with, DO NOT look at the story on the page below. Fill in the blanks on this page with the words called for. Then, using the words you have selected, fill in the blank spaces in the story.

Now you've created your own hilarious MAD LIBS® game!

CLASS PHOTO

SOMETHING ALIVE _____

ADJECTIVE _____

NUMBER _____

NOUN _____

PLURAL NOUN _____

PART OF THE BODY (PLURAL) _____

VERB _____

ARTICLE OF CLOTHING _____

PART OF THE BODY _____

PART OF THE BODY _____

YOUR NAME _____

PERSON YOU KNOW _____

CELEBRITY _____

NUMBER _____

SILLY WORD _____

EXCLAMATION _____

PART OF THE BODY _____

ADJECTIVE _____

MAD LIBS®

CLASS PHOTO

Hey, students at _____ Elementary School! Let's take your
              SOMETHING ALIVE

_____ class picture! Please line up in _____ rows and
ADJECTIVE   NUMBER

stand on your special _____ . I need to be able to see every
                      NOUN

single student and your big, beautiful _____ . Remember
                                 PLURAL NOUN

to stand up straight and keep your _____ to
                             PART OF THE BODY (PLURAL)

your sides. Please don't _____ too much. Student wearing
                      VERB

the bright red _____ , can you please take your
               ARTICLE OF CLOTHING

_____ out of your _____ ? And _____ ,
PART OF THE BODY   PART OF THE BODY   YOUR NAME

please move a little closer to _____ . _____ ,
                      PERSON YOU KNOW   CELEBRITY

can you position yourself to the left of your class? Now on the count

of _____ , look at me and say " _____ !"
      NUMBER   SILLY WORD

_____ ! Now, let's take one more—everyone stick out your
EXCLAMATION

_____ and strike a/an _____ pose!
PART OF THE BODY   ADJECTIVE

From I'M 9, EVERYTHING'S FINE MAD LIBS® • Copyright © 2023 by Penguin Random House LLC

MAD LIBS® is fun to play with friends, but you can also play it by yourself! To begin with, DO NOT look at the story on the page below. Fill in the blanks on this page with the words called for. Then, using the words you have selected, fill in the blank spaces in the story.

Now you've created your own hilarious MAD LIBS® game!

SOCCER IS SUPER!

ANIMAL (PLURAL) _____

A PLACE _____

CITY _____

PLURAL NOUN _____

NUMBER _____

ADJECTIVE _____

PERSON YOU KNOW _____

PART OF THE BODY (PLURAL) _____

VERB ENDING IN "ING" _____

CELEBRITY _____

YOUR NAME _____

VERB ENDING IN "ING" _____

OCCUPATION _____

PART OF THE BODY _____

NOUN _____

ADJECTIVE _____

Today's a big day for my soccer team, the Mighty _____.
                                                    ANIMAL (PLURAL)

We've traveled all the way to (the) _____ to play the
                                     A PLACE

championship game against the East _____ _____.
                                       CITY   PLURAL NOUN

The first half of the game is close, and the score is tied at _____.
                                                               NUMBER

But during the second half of the game, our team makes a lot of

_____ mistakes. _____ and I crash into each other
  ADJECTIVE   PERSON YOU KNOW

and we almost break our _____. Then a player from
                         PART OF THE BODY (PLURAL)

the other team steals the ball and starts _____ all
                                            VERB ENDING IN "ING"

the way across the field. Coach _____ calls a time-out.
                                     CELEBRITY

" _____," the coach says. "You need to use your special
   YOUR NAME

move, the _____ spin-and-kick." The _____
           VERB ENDING IN "ING"   OCCUPATION

blows the whistle and the game starts again. I strike the ball as hard

as I can with my _____. It goes in the _____! The
                  PART OF THE BODY   NOUN

crowd goes _____! Gooooooooooal!
            ADJECTIVE

From I'M 9, EVERYTHING'S FINE MAD LIBS® • Copyright © 2023 by Penguin Random House LLC

MAD LIBS® is fun to play with friends, but you can also play it by yourself! To begin with, DO NOT look at the story on the page below. Fill in the blanks on this page with the words called for. Then, using the words you have selected, fill in the blank spaces in the story.

Now you've created your own hilarious MAD LIBS® game!

BAND PRACTICE

VERB ENDING IN "ING" _____

PART OF THE BODY (PLURAL) _____

CITY _____

TYPE OF BUILDING _____

NOUN _____

ANIMAL _____

NUMBER _____

NOUN _____

OCCUPATION _____

CELEBRITY _____

SAME CELEBRITY _____

ARTICLE OF CLOTHING (PLURAL) _____

PERSON YOU KNOW _____

PLURAL NOUN _____

SAME PERSON YOU KNOW _____

PLURAL NOUN _____

OCCUPATION _____

PLURAL NOUN _____

MAD LIBS®

BAND PRACTICE

Taylor: The first concert for our new band, the _____
VERB ENDING IN "ING"

_____ , is next week at the _____
PART OF THE BODY (PLURAL)   CITY

_____ and we're not ready!
TYPE OF BUILDING

Harry: I know. My _____ sounds like a dying _____ .
NOUN   ANIMAL

Taylor: We need to rehearse, like, _____ more times. You know
NUMBER

the saying: "Practice makes _____ ."
NOUN

Harry: And we need a new _____ , too.
OCCUPATION

Taylor: How about _____ ?
CELEBRITY

Harry: I think _____ may be too busy shopping for new
SAME CELEBRITY

_____ .
ARTICLE OF CLOTHING (PLURAL)

Taylor: I bet _____ plays the _____ and could
PERSON YOU KNOW   PLURAL NOUN

do a good job!

Harry: Yes, _____ would be the answer to our
SAME PERSON YOU KNOW

_____ . But they just got hired to be the newest _____
PLURAL NOUN   OCCUPATION

for the Rolling _____ !
PLURAL NOUN

MAD LIBS® is fun to play with friends, but you can also play it by yourself! To begin with, DO NOT look at the story on the page below. Fill in the blanks on this page with the words called for. Then, using the words you have selected, fill in the blank spaces in the story.

Now you've created your own hilarious MAD LIBS® game!

ROLLER COASTER MANIA

NUMBER _____

VERB ENDING IN "ING" _____

ANIMAL _____

NOUN _____

PART OF THE BODY _____

OCCUPATION _____

PART OF THE BODY (PLURAL) _____

VEHICLE _____

NUMBER _____

A PLACE _____

PART OF THE BODY (PLURAL) _____

SILLY WORD _____

NUMBER _____

ADJECTIVE _____

EXCLAMATION _____

TYPE OF LIQUID _____

ARTICLE OF CLOTHING _____

NUMBER _____

MAD LIBS

ROLLER COASTER MANIA

Now that I'm _____ inches tall, I can ride the world's fastest,
                  NUMBER

scariest roller coaster, the Super _____ _____ .
                                  VERB ENDING IN "ING"   ANIMAL

The best seat is right in the _____ . As I strap a safety belt
                              NOUN

over my _____ , the _____ reminds everyone,
        PART OF THE BODY   OCCUPATION

"Please keep your _____ inside the _____
                  PART OF THE BODY (PLURAL)   VEHICLE

at all times." Soon, the roller coaster is climbing _____ feet in the
                                                     NUMBER

air. I'm so high up, I can see all the way to (the) _____ ! Then
                                                   A PLACE

I close my _____ and scream " _____ "
           PART OF THE BODY (PLURAL)   SILLY WORD

as the roller coaster plunges down. It loops upside down _____
                                                         NUMBER

times in row and then races inside a dark, _____ tunnel.
                                           ADJECTIVE

When the roller coaster comes out of the tunnel, it jerks to the right

and— _____ ! It splashes down into _____ .
     EXCLAMATION   TYPE OF LIQUID

My _____ is soaking wet as the roller coaster comes
   ARTICLE OF CLOTHING

to a complete stop. Can we ride it _____ more times?
                                   NUMBER

MAD LIBS® is fun to play with friends, but you can also play it by yourself! To begin with, DO NOT look at the story on the page below. Fill in the blanks on this page with the words called for. Then, using the words you have selected, fill in the blank spaces in the story.

Now you've created your own hilarious MAD LIBS® game!

THE CUTEST, MOST ADORABLE PET EVER

ANIMAL (PLURAL) _____

PERSON YOU KNOW _____

PART OF THE BODY _____

ADJECTIVE _____

VERB _____

ADJECTIVE _____

VERB _____

PLURAL NOUN _____

ADJECTIVE _____

PART OF THE BODY _____

PERSON YOU KNOW _____

COLOR _____

CELEBRITY _____

ANIMAL _____

ADJECTIVE _____

NUMBER _____

MAD LIBS
THE CUTEST, MOST ADORABLE PET EVER

I like cute _____ and I cannot lie.
ANIMAL (PLURAL)

_____ might see one and say "Bye!"
PERSON YOU KNOW

But when I spot its adorable _____, I melt with joy!
PART OF THE BODY

I feel a/an _____ urge to _____ it
ADJECTIVE   _VERB_

a/an _____ toy!
ADJECTIVE

My pet is so clever, it can _____ on command;
VERB

if I need some _____, I don't have to demand.
PLURAL NOUN

If something _____ happens and I feel sad,
ADJECTIVE

I can pet its soft _____ so I don't feel so bad.
PART OF THE BODY

_____ may have a/an _____ cat;
PERSON YOU KNOW   _COLOR_

_____ may have a pet _____ with a hat.
CELEBRITY   _ANIMAL_

But my pet is as cute and as _____ as can be,
ADJECTIVE

my no. _____ pet is the perfect one for me!
NUMBER

From I'M 9, EVERYTHING'S FINE MAD LIBS® • Copyright © 2023 by Penguin Random House LLC

MAD LIBS® is fun to play with friends, but you can also play it by yourself! To begin with, DO NOT look at the story on the page below. Fill in the blanks on this page with the words called for. Then, using the words you have selected, fill in the blank spaces in the story.

Now you've created your own hilarious MAD LIBS® game!

I SCREAM FOR ICE CREAM

NOUN _____

TYPE OF FOOD _____

ADJECTIVE _____

TYPE OF LIQUID _____

TYPE OF FOOD (PLURAL) _____

NUMBER _____

TYPE OF CONTAINER _____

COLOR _____

TYPE OF FOOD _____

PERSON YOU KNOW _____

TYPE OF LIQUID _____

TYPE OF FOOD _____

COLOR _____

NUMBER _____

TYPE OF LIQUID _____

NOUN _____

EXCLAMATION _____

PART OF THE BODY _____

MAD LIBS®

I SCREAM FOR ICE CREAM

On special occasions like _____'s Day or National

_____ Day, my family and I always make a/an _____
TYPE OF FOOD   ADJECTIVE

treat: homemade ice-cream sundaes! We mix _____ with
TYPE OF LIQUID

several spoonfuls of _____ and freeze it overnight at
TYPE OF FOOD (PLURAL)

_____ degrees. The next day, we scoop the frozen ice cream into
NUMBER

a/an _____ and add our favorite toppings! I like to add
TYPE OF CONTAINER

_____ sprinkles and crumbled _____ cookies.
COLOR   TYPE OF FOOD

_____ likes to pour lots of dark _____ all
PERSON YOU KNOW   TYPE OF LIQUID

over the ice cream. Sometimes we make one big _____
TYPE OF FOOD

split for the entire family to share. We cut up a/an _____
COLOR

banana, add _____ scoops of ice cream, squirt on a mound
NUMBER

of fluffy whipped _____, and top it with a big, round
TYPE OF LIQUID

red _____. _____! Just looking at it makes
NOUN   EXCLAMATION

my _____ water. Time to dig in!
PART OF THE BODY

From I'M 9, EVERYTHING'S FINE MAD LIBS® • Copyright © 2023 by Penguin Random House LLC

MAD LIBS® is fun to play with friends, but you can also play it by yourself! To begin with, DO NOT look at the story on the page below. Fill in the blanks on this page with the words called for. Then, using the words you have selected, fill in the blank spaces in the story.

Now you've created your own hilarious MAD LIBS® game!

A VERY CHALLENGING MATH PROBLEM

PERSON YOU KNOW _____

TYPE OF FOOD _____

A PLACE _____

NUMBER _____

VEHICLE _____

FIRST NAME _____

NUMBER _____

TYPE OF BUILDING _____

NUMBER _____

NOUN _____

NOUN _____

A PLACE _____

CELEBRITY _____

VEHICLE _____

ARTICLE OF CLOTHING (PLURAL) _____

TYPE OF EVENT _____

SAME TYPE OF FOOD _____

NUMBER _____

MAD LIBS®
A VERY CHALLENGING
MATH PROBLEM

_____ has a sudden urge to have _____ for
PERSON YOU KNOW   TYPE OF FOOD

dinner tonight, which is only available at a/an _____ that
                                                        A PLACE

is _____ miles away. They jump in a/an _____ and
     NUMBER   VEHICLE

pick up _____, who lives exactly _____ miles away in
            FIRST NAME   NUMBER

a/an _____. Together, they travel at _____ miles
          TYPE OF BUILDING   NUMBER

per hour, or as fast as a speeding _____. But halfway
                                            NOUN

there, the _____ suddenly breaks, and they're stranded
                    NOUN

in the middle of (the) _____. Just as all hope is lost,
                              A PLACE

_____ drives by in a fancy _____ and invites them
    CELEBRITY   VEHICLE

to hop on board. But first they have to get dressed up in designer

_____ and make a brief appearance at a/an
ARTICLE OF CLOTHING (PLURAL)

_____. When they finally reach the restaurant, it's about
    TYPE OF EVENT

to close, but they're told they can order as much _____
                                                        SAME TYPE OF FOOD

as they want, and it will cost as much as the number of miles they

traveled. How much did they pay for their food? Answer: _____
                                                              NUMBER

dollars.

From I'M 9, EVERYTHING'S FINE MAD LIBS® • Copyright © 2023 by Penguin Random House LLC

MAD LIBS® is fun to play with friends, but you can also play it by yourself! To begin with, DO NOT look at the story on the page below. Fill in the blanks on this page with the words called for. Then, using the words you have selected, fill in the blank spaces in the story.

Now you've created your own hilarious MAD LIBS® game!

DEAR DIARY

ADJECTIVE _____

TYPE OF FOOD _____

ANIMAL _____

TYPE OF LIQUID _____

NOUN _____

NUMBER _____

COLOR _____

PART OF THE BODY (PLURAL) _____

PART OF THE BODY (PLURAL) _____

SILLY WORD _____

OCCUPATION _____

NOUN _____

PLURAL NOUN _____

A PLACE _____

CELEBRITY _____

PART OF THE BODY (PLURAL) _____

VERB ENDING IN "ING" _____

PLURAL NOUN _____

MAD LIBS®

DEAR DIARY

Dear Diary,

Today started as a/an _____ day. I woke up and ate a hearty
                             ADJECTIVE

breakfast of _____ . Then I took my pet _____ for
          TYPE OF FOOD   ANIMAL

a walk around the neighborhood. Suddenly, I stepped in a puddle of

sticky, smelly _____ . I looked up and saw an unidentified
           TYPE OF LIQUID

flying _____ descend from the sky. A creature with _____
        NOUN   NUMBER

_____ _____ stepped out. It looked
     COLOR   PART OF THE BODY (PLURAL)

me straight in the _____ and said, "Greetings,
               PART OF THE BODY (PLURAL)

_____! We are searching for a/an _____ to help
    SILLY WORD   OCCUPATION

us fix our space- _____ . As you can see, it is leaking
             NOUN

and dropping _____ on unsuspecting people's heads."
         PLURAL NOUN

I said, "I'd be glad to help. You need to go to the local auto repair

_____ and ask for _____!" The creature nodded its
   A PLACE   CELEBRITY

_____ , and in a flash, the _____
 PART OF THE BODY (PLURAL)   VERB ENDING IN "ING"

spaceship disappeared into the _____ .
                        PLURAL NOUN

From I'M 9, EVERYTHING'S FINE MAD LIBS® • Copyright © 2023 by Penguin Random House LLC

MAD LIBS® is fun to play with friends, but you can also play it by yourself! To begin with, DO NOT look at the story on the page below. Fill in the blanks on this page with the words called for. Then, using the words you have selected, fill in the blank spaces in the story.

Now you've created your own hilarious MAD LIBS® game!

THE BEST FIELD TRIP EVER

ADJECTIVE _____

PERSON YOU KNOW _____

VEHICLE _____

SILLY WORD _____

NUMBER _____

COLOR _____

NUMBER _____

ANIMAL _____

PART OF THE BODY (PLURAL) _____

CELEBRITY _____

ADJECTIVE _____

ANIMAL _____

VERB _____

NOUN _____

TYPE OF FOOD _____

EXCLAMATION _____

PART OF THE BODY _____

ARTICLE OF CLOTHING _____

MAD LIBS

THE BEST FIELD TRIP EVER

Today, I went on the most _____ field trip ever! I sat next to
ADJECTIVE

my friend _____ as we rode a big yellow _____
PERSON YOU KNOW   VEHICLE

and sang _____ songs all the way there. After more
SILLY WORD

than _____ hours, we finally arrived at the Aquarium of the
NUMBER

_____ Ocean. Inside the aquarium, there were more than
COLOR

_____ underwater creatures, like a glow-in-the-dark _____
NUMBER   ANIMAL

with eight _____ that swam in a tank taller than I
PART OF THE BODY (PLURAL)

am. A volunteer named _____ led us on a/an _____
CELEBRITY   ADJECTIVE

tour. We touched a spiky sea _____, watched penguins
ANIMAL

_____ around, and learned about how to protect our
VERB

precious _____. We even took turns feeding _____
NOUN   TYPE OF FOOD

to a bunch of hungry sharks. _____! When it was my
EXCLAMATION

turn, the shark jumped up and almost bit off my _____!
PART OF THE BODY

It was a very close call! But luckily, it missed chewing on my favorite

_____ .
ARTICLE OF CLOTHING

From I'M 9, EVERYTHING'S FINE MAD LIBS® • Copyright © 2023 by Penguin Random House LLC

MAD LIBS® is fun to play with friends, but you can also play it by yourself! To begin with, DO NOT look at the story on the page below. Fill in the blanks on this page with the words called for. Then, using the words you have selected, fill in the blank spaces in the story.

Now you've created your own hilarious MAD LIBS® game!

MY ROBOT

PART OF THE BODY (PLURAL) _____

ADJECTIVE _____

NUMBER _____

VERB (PAST TENSE) _____

COLOR _____

ADJECTIVE _____

NOUN _____

PART OF THE BODY _____

CELEBRITY _____

VERB _____

ARTICLE OF CLOTHING (PLURAL) _____

NUMBER _____

ADJECTIVE _____

LETTER OF THE ALPHABET _____

ADJECTIVE _____

EXCLAMATION _____

MAD LIBS

MY ROBOT

I've always wanted a robot that looked just like me and had the same

beautiful _____ I do. My wish came true yesterday
_{PART OF THE BODY (PLURAL)}

when a/an _____ package arrived on my doorstep. Inside
_{ADJECTIVE}

were more than _____ tiny pieces that could be put together
_{NUMBER}

to make my very own robot! I carefully _____ the
_{VERB (PAST TENSE)}

instructions. First I connected all the _____ pieces to the
_{COLOR}

_____ pieces. Then I glued the _____ securely
_{ADJECTIVE} _{NOUN}

to the _____ . But then, somehow, the robot began
_{PART OF THE BODY}

to look like _____ . It was so awful that I wanted to
_{CELEBRITY}

_____ forever. Instead, I took a deep breath, rolled up my
_{VERB}

_____ , and started all over again. It took me
_{ARTICLE OF CLOTHING (PLURAL)}

more than _____ hours, but I finally completed my _____
_{NUMBER} _{ADJECTIVE}

masterpiece. Finally, I activated the robot by installing two double

_____ batteries and pressing the _____ button.
_{LETTER OF THE ALPHABET} _{ADJECTIVE}

_____! My robot double is alive!
_{EXCLAMATION}

From I'M 9, EVERYTHING'S FINE MAD LIBS® • Copyright © 2023 by Penguin Random House LLC

MAD LIBS® is fun to play with friends, but you can also play it by yourself! To begin with, DO NOT look at the story on the page below. Fill in the blanks on this page with the words called for. Then, using the words you have selected, fill in the blank spaces in the story.

Now you've created your own hilarious MAD LIBS® game!

RULES FOR BEING 9

NUMBER _____

PART OF THE BODY (PLURAL) _____

VERB ENDING IN "ING" _____

ARTICLE OF CLOTHING _____

PART OF THE BODY _____

NUMBER _____

ADJECTIVE _____

TYPE OF LIQUID _____

NUMBER _____

PART OF THE BODY (PLURAL) _____

SILLY WORD _____

OCCUPATION _____

ANIMAL _____

TYPE OF FOOD _____

ADVERB _____

NOUN _____

PERSON YOU KNOW _____

MAD LIBS®

RULES FOR BEING 9

Here are some important rules for anyone who's _____ years old:

NUMBER

- **Do** wash carefully behind your _____ while

PART OF THE BODY (PLURAL)

  _____.

VERB ENDING IN "ING"

- **Do** wear a/an _____ on your head to protect your

ARTICLE OF CLOTHING

  _____ from the sun.

PART OF THE BODY

- **Do** sleep at least _____ hours a night so that you feel

NUMBER

  _____ in the morning.

ADJECTIVE

- **Don't** drink _____ after _____ o'clock!

TYPE OF LIQUID   NUMBER

- **Do** proudly wave your _____ in the air and

PART OF THE BODY (PLURAL)

  yell _____ after you finish your homework.

SILLY WORD

- **Don't** tell your _____ that the _____ ate your

OCCUPATION   ANIMAL

  homework.

- **Do** spend your ninth year eating all the _____ you

TYPE OF FOOD

  want, _____ singing your favorite song, "Somewhere

ADVERB

  Over the _____," and hanging out with _____!

NOUN   PERSON YOU KNOW

From I'M 9, EVERYTHING'S FINE MAD LIBS® • Copyright © 2023 by Penguin Random House LLC

Download Mad Libs today!

Join the millions of Mad Libs fans
creating wacky and wonderful
stories on our apps!